PANDEMONIUM

ARMANDO IANNUCCI

PANDEMONIUM

Some Verses on the Current Predicament

With illustrations by
Andy Riley

Little, Brown

LITTLE, BROWN

First published in Great Britain in 2021 by Little, Brown

1 3 5 7 9 10 8 6 4 2

Illustrations by Andy Riley

A CIP catalogue record for this book
is available from the British Library.

ISBN 978-1-4087-1508-6

Typeset in Palatino by M Rules
Printed and bound in Great Britain by
Clays Ltd, Elcograf S.p.A.

Papers used by Little, Brown are from well-managed forests
and other responsible sources.

Little, Brown
An imprint of
Little, Brown Book Group
Carmelite House
50 Victoria Embankment
London EC4Y 0DZ

An Hachette UK Company
www.hachette.co.uk

www.littlebrown.co.uk

'This horror will grow mild, this darkness light.'

Paradise Lost, Book 2, line 220

CONTENTS

PANDEMONIUM

INTRODUCTION

S ay, heaving Muse, what catalogue of restraints
And luckless lockdowns fell upon th'unwilling world
Accompanied by pain and stifled shouts of family grief
Till the world's wisest company of brethren
In stately halls and candelabra'd chambers flush
At their desks with freshest data
Brought an end to that wailing noise
And comfort to those begging for release.

Tell, Mighty Wit, how the highest in forethought and,
That tremendous plus, the Science,   10
Saw off our panic and globed vexation
Until a drape of calmness furled around the earth
And beckoned a new and greater normal into each life
For which we give plenty gratitude and pay
Willingly for the vict'ry triumph
Merited by these wisest Gods.

Take us bravely to that source of all our woe,
A wet and withered bat in Wuhan, or, some say,
A bat-lab nearby, carelessly venting bat juice to the world
While, 'tis equally true, Pharma and/or Bill Gates,   20
In league with Illuminati lizards,
Hid poisoned cameras in our breath
So we could spray their malice drop by drop
Like spoken mist, as from a tower of Babel
Or like that other mighty shaft, the mast of 5G
(For, yes, I near forgot, 5G is another cause,
Since everyone has seen it said,
Where G is for George, and 5, to all, is clearly S,
The sign of the malevolent serpent Soros, it is true.)
And all is truth, for truth also can mutate,   30
Into twenty truths, and spawn twenty variants more,
Once uttered, slotting any gaping void of sense
And fitting it like a fisting fact.

PART 1

T ell first of one who fought that bat, and tackled truth
  As it clawed and ravaged his beating lungs
And near ended life in some ventilated corner
Of a ward. Orbis Rex was he known on high
By all the Gods, 'World King' by birth and plan,
Though the Gods, sensing men would stall in fear
Of his breeding, transformed 'Orbis' to more earthly 'Boris',   40
Spurring love and laughter from us on hearing
This more mortal name.

Say how this hero Boris, seeming felled
By the evil mite, coughed back up
His gleaming soul renewed and rode out to fight
Sadness with mirth, and brought lilting light
Into the darkest streets and homes of his kingdom.
Golden capped, like a sainted knight, he slew that dragon
In twelve weeks or so, or if not weeks then months,

And if not slew then tossed it flattened   50
Back into its cave, where it would certainly
Think long and hard before it dared to spaff
Its deadly spew upon this land again
And spread its dark and manic ills.

Go back to that day, when the bat first smote Europe
And he, our Hero, to lull it into thinking us unprepared
Deliberately sat at home, in a country house, finishing
A book, and gathering his family in games and sport
Lest the bat gain sense of how ready he was,
(A feint he learnt on rugby's field).   60
Then, luring that flying fury across our shore
And into these islands, this hero struck and fell
Upon his friend Hancock, also known as Matt,
Which, as any mat splayed upon the ground
Gives surface protection to feet that stamp
Upon his front and welcome smiles
To those who enter their domain
And drop their dirt, gave Orbis full grace.

'Dear Friend,' spake Bojo, for so this immortal being
In earthly guise was also known, 'as you are a friend   70

And will vouch for anything I subsequently do,
And publicly vamp with reasoned praise my actions
And defend with utmost cleverness any wise delay
I might cunningly effect, so now I turn to you,
Sweet Friend, and ask for Friendship's suckle.
Help me, please, my Matt. In Christ's name
Summon all the friends you can!'

Lo, before another second fell into oblivion's well
Matt roared to attention and sputtered gladly: 'Sire,
Friendship is our strength and so shall be our success.   80
Friendship's Circle is where our Vict'ry lies
And I will journey swiftly there to pluck what's best
I can from that great engorging pile.'
With immediate effect, Matt mounted his beast
(For fabulous riding skills he possessed and firmly
Wielded a jockey's crop) and galloped like a dart
To where the circle lay.

PART 2

How can I describe with imperfect tongue that sewer
Of rank and rabid fervour, the Circle of Friends
Who lay, writhing flanks and limbs entangled,   90
Like a clump of worms gathered by a fisherman
And placed in ready bucket for his line,
So these Friends coagulated round themselves,
Each one bait for another, bait upon bait,
Knowing one another and each one known,
Till they knew themselves inside out,
Arses eaten by faces, faeces dropped on eyes,
Arms reaching into guts, lips retching hands out whole,
Bodies intimate and knotted like a dungy braid.

'Hi,' said Matt, jumping from his steed and onto heads   100
Of slithering companions. 'I need your help.'
The ball of colleagues writhed as one,
And a string of fifteen twats and ani formed a mouth.

'Gladly,' they unisoned, in a gasp of tears and pain,
'Take some of us from this hellish mix-up
And give us purpose and reward. We will not
Fail you, or, if we do, it shall be for reasons
Understandable.'

Matt approached his horse and pushed it to the side.
'No need have I for this feckless mare   110
When I can ride my Friends far faster
To Vict'ry's Ball, where I shall stake my face
As that master jockey of events, in thrall
To no one, nay, not even Orbis and all his claims.'
With that, the congealed and muddy pile of amity
Rose up as one, a thread of cadavers knit by need
Into the shape of a magnificent Beast.

Some say 'twas like a horse, others that a bird it formed,
But most would say that no words could describe
That ghastly, foul and lolloping creature,   120
So crazily did its limbs and offal conform,
A composit pack of body parts contriving to a whole.
'Friends, Contacts, Colleagues and Mates, I call
Upon ye to ride rescue of our parlous state

And rid the world of this thieving sickness,'
Said Matt, as he mounted the Beast of Bits.
'But wait,' he cried, 'there is no head!'

His words were true. The compounded animal
Had limbs and stomach, buttocks and flanks
But no head to crown its composition.   130
'The neck is strong, I give you that, but just ends
Puckered incomplete. Give me a head to finish the form
And put a face on our inevitable success.'
'Choose me!' said one, left as scraps
In the stomach of another on the ground.
'Leave me not, like one who left me long ago
Never to return. For I am Dido, forsaken by Aeneas
And left to rot. Remember me!
Remember me, for evermore!
Put my pate on your colleagues' pile of limbs   140
And let me be your wisdom's gleaming crown!'

'You are Dido, and as Dido, have become my Queen,'
Said Matt, placing her atop his bastardised pet,
'And as Dido you'll be known for evermore,
For surely no one will forget your name.'

So, crouching to the noggin, he picked her up
And stitched her laughing to his mare of mates.
And then laughed all there in their merry panoply,
Shining hope where darkness lay.

PART 3

But hold!   150

What of the foul and stinking fiend the virus?
Did it flinch to hear what Force would soon arrive
And staunch its merciless flow? No, no noise
It made, and in unfair silence it cast its pall
Across the fields of old and ill; into the chambers
Of the mighty and the powerless its fluid ran
And suffocated all smiles and embraces of the young,
Snatching any hope from the hearts of the weary
And the strong. And silence fell like drifts of snow
Across the realm, or, if not snow, then ash.   160
And all withdrew in fear and grief into their hearths
And homes, their beloved and latest loves,
As quietly we waited for the assault long told.

And in silence too all grief was sung.
In distant whispers, alone or with a few,

A coffin the one unmasked cry of anger
At the loss, stilled by those distant farewells,
Kisses on screens and goodbyes by broadband
Which pulse across the fields and into
The sorrowful moment until all is mute.   170

But, rush! There came a noise, whose firm sense
And hollering uplifted hearts in every house. 'Folks!'
Said Orbis Rex, 'We face an enemy unwelcome,
Whom we shall fight with every sinew we can spare.
For let our watchword be "Hurrah!" And "No More!"'
Orbis stood in a mighty chamber newly raised
Reflecting all his glory, rebounding off
Teak panelling and glorious carpets. 'Fantastically,'
He cried, 'we shall put on our armour, or,
If none available, improvise with sheets and cladding,   180
Or cloth barriers and plastic bags, or paper
If need be, or pulp. The point is:
We are ready! Fantastic!'

Next to Orbis stood twin magnificent angels,
Strong in wisdom and wise in facts.
Sweetness and Light were their names,

And from them shone unreflected sense and caution too.
'I concur with Orbis and all he says,' spoke Sweetness,
'Though Science suggests I fleshen out his words
So they may make more digestible sense.   190
We are not ready. At least not yet.' 'Agreed,'
Added Light. 'But if we were equipped with every
Mode of repulsion, every cape and gown,
Every datum and science in the land,
Then, yes, we would be ready, is what he said.'

'It's fantastic you agree,' said Orbis, swelling wide,
'And fantastic too the future waiting for us
If we snatch the victor's goblet from Pandemic's mouth.
So I say, We will ride out and rid this realm
Of any wretch that impedes our life. We will tell it   200
That after twelve weeks it must begone, and it will heed
My words, for they are as nifty as ghosts in flight, and can
Scuttle any mortal threat. We are Great, and, if not Great
Then getting near it, and so we tell this vermin to vamoose!'

'Ha ha!' cried everyone. 'Vamoose! Though we are in pain
We can also laugh at this speech's alliterative effect.
'Vamoose! Ha ha!' Though others were mute,

Unmoved yet by those sparkling words, waiting
For their full benediction to fall on them,
Which they knew would be soon, since hope   210
Was now sprouting across the land. And 'Ha!'
And 'Ha!' again came a shout from up the hill
As Hancock and his ball of contacts galloped
Upon its brow and down into the Vale of Death.

PART 4

Muses grant me strength to tell the unspeakable,
For words can't express how Orbis and his company
Fought that Pandemic, and like a miracle, if
Miracles defy all human intellect and fact,
Won eternal glory undisputed. But how?
Tell first of Matt's charge into the dark valley   220
Upon his Beast of Bits. 'Advance!' he cried, though
In that cry a smile, as if knowing vict'ry was nigh
And he would bring mirth back to these shores,
Supplanting Orbis in the nation's love. Alas,
For him a muted glory.

                      As he rode the gory creature,
Each flank shouted its own knowledge, in several squawks.
'I know someone in Coventry,' said a knee, 'who works
In manufacturing, I think. Maybe he can source
Us capes and gowns and other armour. He's called Nick.'   230

'I too know a Nick, in Kent,' said a bit of neck, 'who
Mentioned masks to me on a drive to Twickenham.
I'll summon him and his mighty produce and together
We will vanquish this poisonous fiend from our land
At a reasonable price, though it may have been casks,
Not masks, he talked about, since he ran a pub,
But worth a try.' And so each portion of the beast
Set its own direction, unhooking from the whole.
Hancock wobbled as the ghastly form shrunk,
Like jelly in the heat, into separate joints and giblets   240
Or as some Lego tower or fortress, mighty and solid,
Is shattered by the surly brother's kick
Into pointless and bepimpled bricks.

'Stay,' said Matt. 'Have my back and hold my bottom,
Fight the fiend as one!' But one became a thousand
Shrieking out confusion all around. 'What do I do and
What do I know?' said one. 'I have no aptitude for this crisis,'
Another. 'I'll do what I can but I'm just a head,' said Dido.
'And that's not my fault!' So tears of utter inability
Flooded from the form and yawning howls perplexed   250
Thrummed throughout the vale.

Matt's lips gawped,
Opening one more time to hurl his inspirations
At the juddering mound of contacts and mates.
But as he pondered what to say he slowly sank
Into their widening pool of mucus and muscles,
Gristle gurgling round his neck, him choking on a thumb,
Others' flanks folding over him, his legs gripped by guts
Of acquaintances, a shoulder dislocated downwards
Into a vortex of bits. One last heave resurfaced him   260
As he spewed a howl for help, begging all to gather back,
His face an open gob of fear.

When sudden! Another face rises!
Gina by name, who, like a mollusc to a tugboat, sucked
And fixed its mouth to his. So two faces became one,
Cheeks merged, and eyeballs compressed in contact,
Tongues entwined, as sprats wrestling in a heron's gullet,
That last image unforgettable as she yanked him down
Into the hypothermic depths of liquid inability
And Matt's once glorious form vanished like a chimera   270
Or a bubble, popped for ever in a dank and futile lake of pals,
Vowing still to re-appear, though in fact he never would.

PART 5

S ay now, what of Orbis? Muses press my mind to tell
Of the mighty battle the snow-capped wonderling won.
But speak first of his darkest hour, as Orbis stood alone
Awaiting Pandemic, ready to meet him on the field.
"Tis best to guard yourself with cloth,' said Sweetness,
Consulting hallowed Graphs and Charts. 'Or so I think.'
'No,' said Light, 'cleanliness will suffice, currently.'
'Fantastic wisdom from you both,' said Orbis, 'but   280
I shall do neither. When Pandemic comes across the field,
Hooting and growling like a beaten dog or a drunken
Character in a Glasgow comedy, I shall disarm him
As I disarm everyone, with my winning smile and charm
Which vents from every pore of my body
And calms the foe remarkably.' With that Orbis sauntered
Like a merry imp, alone to meet the deadly foe.

And towards him rushed a glooming darkness,
A cloud of choking mist where all light ended
And no shades softly landed but rather   290
Were beams of solid shadows, shafting
Indestructible deep into the earth, and where
All brightness in its path was felled by suffocation.

'Pleased to meet you,' said Orbis, stretching out his hand.
'I'm shaking hands with everyone and, as you can see,
I'll do it to you, though far vaster in magnificence
You look to me than I was expecting. You are indeed
A mighty foe, but one with whom I can surely reach
An understanding. Let's do this.' And so shook hands.

What a murmur and a rumbling roar arose upon the land   300
As Pandemic's hand extended round Orbis' form entire
And burst it with a squeeze. At once a sullen oozing sound
Permeated that place, as clouds of charismatic gas escaped,
That once kept Orbis' outward shape sheened and resplendid
Now billowing out to nowhere. Orbis flopped unsustainable
As a man, and fell to deepest sleep, and in that fall
Plumbed the depths of a long, dark well, vertical for ever
And stretching down to an unspoken place, a vault

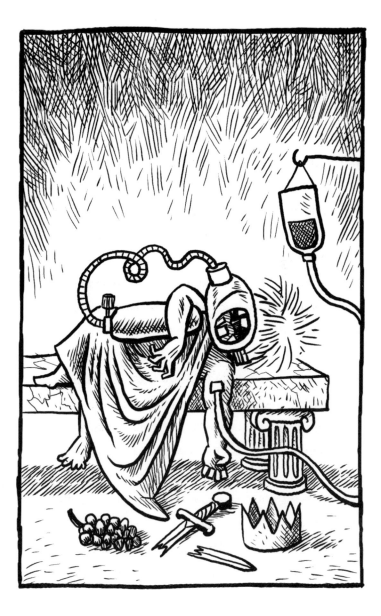

Of never-ending sighs and breaths and beeps and blood,
A cavern hollowed out by fear, yet bringing care to most   310
Connected to wires and pouches of redeeming air.

Orbis lay twixt dreams and life, neither in nor out
His head, but in a strange part-world where only
Silence is heard, and light is touch, and taste is gone
And faces feel familiar though masked, and timelessness
Is chimed by beating clicks and pulses regulated. A void
Yet filled. A death and resurrection equally beckoning.
One he saw there who seemed remembered and yet unknown,
A shape in ghastly yet human form, a wan appearance
As if disappointed evermore, sitting in a cart   320
Drawn by a hundred thousand scurrying creatures,
Mice and bats, insects and rats all pulling
On winches and ropes tethered at the front,
Dragging the battered cart along by demi-inches
Around a pillar, in constant circles wandering,
And the torrid driver stretching out to feel his way
That once was clear but now was gone.

Orbis stood before him and asked the creeping form
'Am I in Hell? And are you the Devil come to take,
By carriage, my protesting soul to its sorry end?'   330

'Ha!' cried the ghoul, 'I'm not Old Nick, but Dom'nic!'
And laughed but nobody laughed with him around
At his flaccid pun. 'My friend, for friend you were
Before: do you not remember my brain
And the wisdom it bestowed?'

                              'No,' said Orbis,
'I have no recollection of who you are.'

                                  'Typical!'
Said Dom'nic. 'For my punishment I am yoked
To a place where my brilliance is camouflaged to nothing   340
And where I'm doomed to be unknown by all, ceaseless
Questing to reach the answer only I can find
But will never do.'

                        'Is that why you use these creatures
To scurry you perpetually, in vain and pitiful circuits?'
Asked Orbis, smiling at the hideous vehicle.

'I once could see,' responded Dom'nic,
'But now am blind. And cursed eternally to test my sight
Around this pillar, powered by these withered creatures,
This claque of rodents and flies in sad formation,   350
Who brought plague into the world, and all its woe.
But they break me not, because I have inner sight
To supplement and supersede my broken eyes.
So let me be your guide to this netherworld
Where all are asleep as in a waking dream,
And I will show you what you cannot see, the world
Around and what madness entered in,
How human hope was whittled to a shrivelled dot,
Yet how human love shines still, enough to light
A whole horizon. Behold, the pain and pity,   360
The pity and the pain.'

PART 6

                    Into the void
Dom'nic looked and squinted, as if surprised
By a glare. Not brightness this, but solid dark
Exploding so that all went dim.

'I can't see!' cried Orbis, squelching on a mouse.
'After all you led me to expect, this is
Disappointment magnified!'

                    'Duff dotard!' cried Dom'nic,
'I alone can see, and can tap your feeble senses   370
So they may grasp what seems invisible.
In our native land, I see before me
A hundred thousand dead, a hundred thousand
Dying, and a thousand thousand lingering
In a stop-frame existence, spent and breathless,

Wond'ring when time will start for them,
Fed suggestions daily, praying for an answer.

'I can hear the ambulances' cries, see the bustle
Of the mortuary, the feverish night in the ward.
I can grasp the fear of the cleaner each dawn.   380
I feel the sudden close of loves just starting,
And hear the tears of the hurt trapped by the hurter.
I freeze at the chill of the choice between food or heat,
And I wish the tenant well who pays only with a plea.

'I see an evil blaze rage through the homes of the old,
Burning lives to the ground, hastening them to ashes
With a roar of lament no one can hear outside.
I see many trapped in mind's melancholy,
As if lost in tunnels of fear and distressing
Expectation.   390

                    'I see someone coughing by a till
But continuing to shop, and the keeper now dead.
I see the florist and the barista no longer active,
The singer silent, the malls muted by shutters,
The father fearful, the mother caged by concern.

I see the sister still at home, unable to travel,
Her brother now dead in another district. I see the nurse
Felled, not by the ward's infected clouds, but
By a passenger, on a bus taken at night
At the end of endless hours.   400

'I witness the paramedic's quandary, ordered
To let elders, fading at home, stay there inside
To rest in peace. I see a Prince's passing
And the ceremony of an empty castle straining
To keep its history alive. I see children bewildered
In their classrooms, preparing for a life they know
Will now be different from what is written down.

'I see hope gaining ground, only to fall at the verge,
And over the horizon, a landscape of loss
And a stillness that hurts, a people reaching   410
Through screens at their untouchable friends,
And summoning family whose nearness seems vast.

'Beyond, I see the world stare at what's coming.
I see first some, then a town and, before an instant
Is out, a country entire disbelieve the data is real

And pray to the Gods to get rid of what's grim
And pivot instead to optimism's tale,
Like contents from a streamer, sure to refresh.

'And inside, I see me, wondering why I am at the centre
Of this ferment, what I did and didn't do, standing   420
Shocked at the speed and the strength of it all, asking
If I did wrong while knowing I did wrong.
I show you these sights, so you too may question
In your heart how soundly you can take down
This foe, and beat it back to the unknown and
The undreaded. Do you see what I see, do you
Feel my hateful realisation of how little
We are against this death-dealing disease?
And against the force of the world beyond us
That we are deaf to, the natural order we dare   430
To think we can enslave? How it outlives us,
Diminishing us by the comparison,
Like mayflies to a tree?'

'Not necessarily,' argued Orbis, and then woke up.

PART 7

S ing of mighty arms! Let the brass horns parp
   At tales of hard-won vict'ry! The battlefield prepped,
Lay silently readied for war. The clamour
Would be hard, the fierce clash obscene,
All were revved with th'utmost energy
To meet their surly foe. But Orbis was hungry,   440
His appetite inflated by sleep's deprivations.
Eager this crash of armies should reach a swift end,
He charged to his throne, ignoring the cleaners
Sanitising it safe for his glorious form.

'Folks, I've got to tell you,' he declaimed to the people
Eager to hear his war-devious plans,
'Stonking progress was achieved in my absence
As by my instruction. I've spoken to someone,
A peculiar fellow, with all of the data,
Who seemed to know a hell of a lot   450

And who taught me to see a thing or two,
Not via dull senses' cache, but with the inner gut
Of the mind. Gazing this way and reading between
The lines, guys, I feel the trajectory is good.'

'There is a long way to go,' said Sweetness.
'We have barely begun,' said Light.
'I think we're nearly there,' said Orbis, 'but with only
A few loose ends to tidy. We've got this,
More or less. I tell you, the virus is pinned to the ground,
Evil's as good as nailed. It's popped its peak.   460
So I say for sanity's sake, all of you please
Come back from the battle, fetch all your purses,
Rejoice in this moment and get out to eat!'

The people were silent, surprised by the speed
Of this total result. As an online delivery
Whose purchase was forgotten, comes sudden
In dead of night, yet sparks quick enjoyment
When opened in the morn, so was the land
Filled with cheer at the surprise and swiftness
Of the unseen victory, and burst with delight.   470
Sensing it safe to emerge, they immediately clamoured

For food at the table, and quaffed with full vim
In a hasty feast. What magnificent chickens
Were roasted that day, how laden were the pizzas
Resumed in their ovens. Hundreds and thousands
Poured Aperol Spritzes, rendered quite massive,
Into a palace of glasses, and up straws like cabers.
Townsfolk gnawed all of Albion's herds,
Wassails were booked and shanties were sung
In riot delicious all over the land.   480

But lo!
What grim endeavour is this, that would catch
Our kin unawares? For Evil's great Sequel
Flooded the boroughs while we were feasting
And brought a second sickness upon us,
More vicious, less original, a mewling
Bastard Badchild cleft from parent's head,
Felling heroes everywhere with its rancid fumes.
'Folks,' spoke Orbis, palely gobsmacked on his throne,
'This vile pestilence has breached the terms   490
Of our agreement fair, and come back at us
Like a toxic charlatan. We maybe
Have to ride again to give it swift dispatch ... '

'We will,' said Sweetness. 'Most certain,' said Light.
'Or maybe not, who knows?' said Orbis, seething
Through his teeth, all flecks of charm dried up
And monumental ire burning in his cheeks.

While willow-capped Orbis stood four-square
The demon grew and grew, its airy sewage
Swaddling the land in knotted pain   500
Until Albion's heart was riven with tears.
'OK, I'll parley once again,' said Orbis, clanking
Armour now shapeless on his form. 'But
This Bastard Badchild must then depart!'
He rode out to seek the fiend, yet all was empty,
The screams of many lifting high, but nothing seen,
Sirens blaring, orderlies shouting, death resumed
In a howling darkness far across the land,
Isolation again encased each home
As winter wandered in.   510

'Folks, all is air and empty.
Bastard Badchild lurks in hiding
Like a busted loser. Why don't we
Shame the ghoul with unexpected chutzpah!

Let's all come out for Christmastime
And, using utmost bravado,
Make Pandemic feel really small!'

The great halls swung open for a second
Hurrah, hope was hysterically high,
As tinsel burst upon the scene,   520
And care homes dreamt of hugs.
When came Sweetness and Light with charts.
'Sire,' said Sweetness, 'Badchild grows apace,
These graphs swell like hillocks. Soon they'll grow
To mountains gigantic, perilous to climb,
Clumsy in the fall.' Orbis swore an oath
And with heaving heavy heart, rode out
A third time to battle, thinking kinsfolk
Years from now, when present melts to past,
Will speak of this encounter as the greatest and the last.   530

FINALE

Many gathered, a stern array of might
In final battle's proud formation,
Retainers and Researchers, brewing
Weapons yet unknown, civilians in their hordes
Asked again to arm themselves with care,
Hospitals at the ready, shoppers fully masked
In armour's brightest cloth.

Orbis Rex, oiled and magnificent,
Wielding statistics' hallowed slides,
Stood centre in the battlefield, and implored: 540
'Once more, fantastic folk, once more,
Let all our fury fly until we find that scourge
Of all our land, and sit it down,
And show it how maddening it has become
And, if not charmed, thump it hard
And send it packing from Albion's shores!'

With one command, 'Ye heroes all, crack on!'
They fired up and bounded out, to charge
At Pandemic's baleful worst. Harsh! Frenzied!
Crack and clash of weapons, howling terror   550
All around! A harrowing like no other
Gripped the land, and armies swooped as one.

Orbis and his troops advantage gained,
And seemed to have command, but soon
Fell back at Pandemic's surging strength.
The monster, joining Bastard Badchild,
Had redoubled its terror, and Albion withdrew.

But, no, what subtle ruse, to lure them both
Near where laboratory archers lay.
In deadly formation, ready to launch   560
A hundred thousand tiny arrows, dashes
Across the skies, each one
Tipped with toxin, stabbing with perfection
The monsters' puking lips and potent groins.

The fiends lolloped back in anger, looking
Likely to fall, when in singular incestuous

Judder, birthed a pool of procreated filth,
A misshapen Variant, stronger than its parents
Who fell spent to the stinking floor.

'Fire those darts, fling needles across the heavens,'   570
Urged Orbis, intent on destruction, inflamed
With apprehension. No sooner had his troops
Advanced, holding the ugly Variant at bay,
When confusion in his ranks upended order.
A parade of Dissenters, dizzy and unbalanced
By constant shaking of their heads, wandered
Across the field, discombobulated from data,
Afflicted with a giddy motion inverting reason,
Seeing hospitals as hateful, and doctors diabolic.

'Show them our slides,' said Light. 'The Science   580
Will win them over.' 'I can't,' said Sweetness.
'They have me in their clutches.
Pray for me, dear Light.' And Sweetness
Was hoisted highward on a board of graphs
And carried by a confused and contrary
Band of dogmatists and dickheads
To a merciless fate in a distant park.

Through the night and morn, both sides raged
In stalemate, equivalent in might,
Arrow upon arrow fell, ping by ping   590
Came back, the Variant wafting
Contact with its form into another five.
Those guided to recovery were matched
By others fallen, each advance
By Orbis' flanks met with more Deviants fresh,
Newly awoken by the call of their infernal
Spawning sire. 'We cannot hold it,'
Shouted Light. 'We must,' said Orbis.
'It's not my fault,' shouted Dido
From a departing car.   600

                    The battle raged
Like Jupiter's spot, all swelling red and
Seeming eternal, the howls and angry pains
From Orbis, Variant, and parading Imbeciles
Professing all to be a charade, mingled
Into an immeasurable roar, until sudden 'Quiet!'
Shouted Orbis. 'This must stop, and if not now,
When will we ever resume our blessed life?'

Undumb was everyone assembled, not
Noiseless their response. 'We need to fly,'   610
Cried Aviators in their fury. 'Death to nurses!'
Shouted a phalanx of Cretins. 'Let us dance!'
Shouted raging Nightclub Owners. 'Heed
The charts,' mumbled Light, searching
In a park. 'It's really not my fault,' re-iterated
Dido, passing in her car. 'We must race again,
Gambling in our thousands!' pleaded Jockeys.
'Quiet yet, I say!' repeated Orbis. 'God's quiet
Must fall upon this earth and command
Our silence.' And silence was there then   620
For once in Albion, as Orbis Rex assumed
His mound and told thus across his realm.

'Folks, fantastic fellows all, pray heed.
This bother has blighted our land but not
Our way of life. I say we have the right to skip
And dance, to flip and fly, and yes, to jest
And jockey! For have we not done so
Already, when we were locked inside
Our houses fabulous? Did we not flit

In the mind, and go on amazing journeys   630
Visually, via Amazon's calming stream?

'Oh the mind, the mind has mountains
Of mirth, and can sustain us with joy.
Even in darkest hours, our imagination
Can turn with untold power one thing
To another, a monkey into the moon,
And buttermilk to gold.

'So, guys, I ask you, is it not within
Our wit to imagine this evil already
Gone? Can we not, like our greatest voice   640
Of stories past, the Shakespearian Bard,
And Dickens too, and all those superb
Scribblers these shores have burped,
Conjure up a happier truth, that already
We have won, and amazingly so?
I am but a man, but you think me marvellous,
Touched by godlihead. You too, I think,
Are utterly brilliant folk, and can inflate
With Albion's wit, what is lowly into
Dazzling flare.   650

'So let us go out again and learn
To live with Dunderhead Disease.
The more we live, the more Terror
Lessens in our thoughts and so begins to die.
If we've faith that we're done with it, then
'Tis done with! Our will, freely used,
Can will sickness from our shores
And paint away these evil days.
So let's gather up our loins and march
Brisk outside, heaving our battle cry   660
With one shout, our forever roar:
"Death thou will be ill; ill, we are alive!"'

All fell silent at these words, pausing
To ingest their sense. A lengthy contemplation
Was required, to harness and enhance
Whate'er they meant. And soon,
With drifting step, we quietly crept out
And back into the world, gaining ground
In confidence to sing and drink.

                          Stories   670

Were started up, of how we slew the monster
And how day resumed as if waking
From a distant sleep. These verses too
Commissioned for my hand,
And other works of supreme art,
Confirmed this truth, that Vict'ry won
Its bravest battle, with Orbis at her helm
Though insistent sickness waits. And while
Some may fall, all are well, if well
Be what seems fit.   680

                    And wielding charm
He won sweet vict'ries more, with cunning
Long gestated from these travails, until
Some time soon after, he took us to the field
Wherein we sensed his surest triumph,
Against the roaring mighty sun. And peace
Returned to Albion's vale, forbidding claims
From any future plagues that might
Stupidly unfurl across this land again,
And tempt us into weakest thoughts   690
That all has fallen ill.

Armando Iannucci is a political commentator, and comedy writer and director. He is the creator of, among others, Alan Partridge, *The Thick of It* and *Veep*. He wrote and directed *The Death of Stalin* and *The Personal History of David Copperfield*.